**AT&T**

ERRATUM
(CORRECTS COVER GRAPHIC)

W9-BKX-873

UNIX® System V

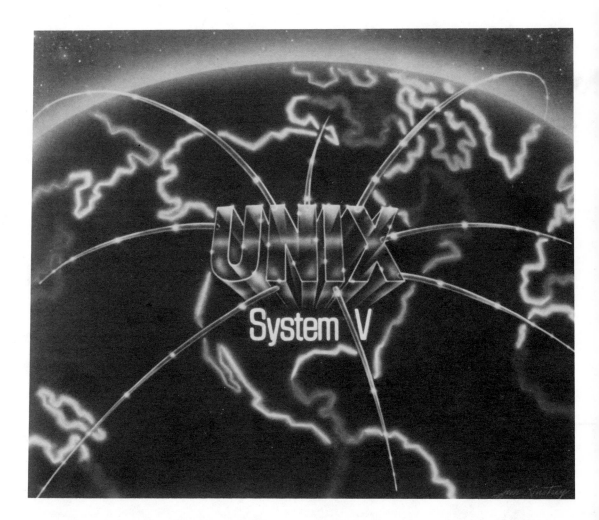

UNIX® System V

STREAMS Primer

AT&T

Prentice-Hall, Inc., Englewood Cliffs, NJ 07632

Library of Congress Catalog Card Number: 87-60152

Editorial/production supervision: Karen S. Fortgang
Cover illustration: Jim Kinstry
Manufacturing buyer: S. Gordon Osbourne

Printed in the United States of America

10 9 8 7 6 5 4 3 2 1

ISBN 0-13-940529-1 025

Prentice-Hall International (UK) Limited, *London*
Prentice-Hall of Australia Pty. Limited, *Sydney*
Editora Prentice-Hall do Brasil, Ltda., *Rio de Janeiro*
Prentice-Hall of Canada Inc., *Toronto*
Prentice-Hall Hispanoamericana, S.A., *Mexico*
Prentice-Hall of India Private Limited, *New Delhi*
Prentice-Hall of Japan, Inc., *Tokyo*
Prentice-Hall of Southeast Asia Pte. Ltd., *Singapore*

Table of Contents

Chapter 5: Kernel Level Functions 29

Chapter 6: Other Facilities 40

Chapter 7: Driver Design Comparisons 55

Glossary 59

1 INTRODUCTION

With the addition of the Networking Support Utilities, UNIX System V Release 3.0 provides comprehensive support for networking services. This *Primer* describes STREAMS, a major building block of that support. The *Primer* provides a high level, technical overview of STREAMS; it is intended for managers and developers who have prior knowledge of the UNIX system and networking or other data communication facilities. For a more detailed description of STREAMS, see the *STREAMS Programmer's Guide* (P-H).

The UNIX system was originally designed as a general-purpose, multi-user, interactive operating system for minicomputers. Initially developed in the 1970's, the system's communications environment included slow to medium speed, asynchronous terminal devices. The original design, the communications environment, and hardware state of the art influenced the character input/output (I/O) mechanism but the character I/O area did not require the same emphasis on modularity and performance as other areas of the system.

Support for a broader range of devices, speeds, modes, and protocols has since been incorporated into the system, but the original character I/O mechanism, which processes one character at a time, made such development difficult. Additionally, a paucity of tools and the absence of a framework for incorporating contemporary networking protocols added to the difficulty.

The current generation of networking protocols is exemplified by Open Systems Interconnection (OSI), Systems Network Architecture (SNA), Transmission Control Protocol/Internet Protocol (TCP/IP), X.25, and Xerox Network Systems (XNS). These protocols provide diverse functionality, layered organization, and various feature options. When developing these protocol suites, developers faced additional problems because there were no relevant standard interfaces in the UNIX system.

Attempts to compensate for the above problems have led to diverse, ad-hoc implementations; for example, protocol drivers are often intertwined with the hardware configuration in which they were developed. As a result, functionally equivalent protocol software often cannot interface with alternate implementations of adjacent protocol layers. Portability, adaptability, and reuse of software have been hindered.

AT&T decided to enhance the character I/O area in Release 3.0. The result is STREAMS, a general, flexible facility and a set of tools for development of UNIX system communication services. With STREAMS, developers can

provide services ranging from complete networking protocol suites to individual device drivers.

STREAMS defines standard interfaces for character I/O within the UNIX kernel, and between the kernel and the rest of the UNIX system. The associated mechanism is simple and open-ended. It consists of a set of system calls, kernel resources, and kernel utility routines. The standard interface and open-ended mechanism enable modular, portable development and easy integration of higher performance network services and their components. STREAMS does not impose any specific network architecture. Instead, it provides a powerful framework with a consistent user interface that is compatible with the existing character I/O interface still available in UNIX System V.

STREAMS modularity and design reflect the "layers and options" characteristics of contemporary networking architectures. The basic components in a STREAMS implementation are referred to as modules. These modules, which reside in the kernel, offer a set of processing functions and associated service interfaces. From user level, modules can be dynamically selected and interconnected to provide any rational processing sequence. Kernel programming, assembly, and link editing are not required to create the interconnection. Modules can also be dynamically "plugged into" existing connections from user level. STREAMS modularity allows:

- User level programs that are independent of underlying protocols and physical communication media.

- Network architectures and higher level protocols that are independent of underlying protocols, drivers, and physical communication media.

- Higher level services that can be created by selecting and connecting lower level services and protocols.

- Enhanced portability of protocol modules resulting from STREAMS' well-defined structure and interface standards.

In addition to modularity, STREAMS provides developers with integral functions, a library of utility routines, and facilities that expedite software design and implementation. The principal facilities are:

- Buffer management – To maintain STREAMS' own, independent buffer pool.

- Flow control – To conserve STREAMS' memory and processing resources.

- Scheduling — To incorporate STREAMS' own scheduling mechanism.

- Multiplexing — For processing interleaved data streams, such as occur in SNA, X.25, and windows.

- Asynchronous operation of STREAMS and user processes — Allows STREAMS-related operations to be performed efficiently from user level.

- Error and trace loggers — For debugging and administrative functions.

STREAMS is the standard for AT&T UNIX system data communications and networking implementations. The original STREAMS concepts were developed in the Information Sciences Research Division of AT&T Bell Laboratories (see "A Stream Input-Output System" in *UNIX System Readings and Applications, Vol. II* (P-H)).

How this Document is Organized

The *Primer* is organized as follows:

- Chapter 2 provides an overview of the applications and benefits of STREAMS and the STREAMS mechanism.

- Chapter 3 describes how to set up a Stream from user level and how this initialization affects the kernel. This and following chapters are aimed at developers.

- Chapter 4 contains a detailed example and discusses it from user level.

- Chapter 5 describes kernel operations associated with the Chapter 4 example, together with a discussion of basic STREAMS kernel facilities.

- Chapter 6 includes kernel and user facilities not otherwise described.

- Chapter 7 compares certain design features of character I/O device drivers with STREAMS modules and drivers.

- The Glossary defines terms that are specific to STREAMS.

Other Documents

The *STREAMS Programmer's Guide* (P-H) contains more detailed STREAMS information for programmers: how programmers can develop networking applications with STREAMS user-level facilities and how system programmers can use STREAMS kernel-level facilities to build modules and drivers.

Section 2 of the *Programmer's Reference Manual* (P-H) and the *System V Interface Definition* (AT&T) include descriptions (manual pages) of STREAMS-related system calls and other information.

2 OVERVIEW

A Basic View of a Stream

"STREAMS" is a collection of system calls, kernel resources, and kernel utility routines that can create, use, and dismantle a "Stream". A Stream is a full-duplex processing and data transfer path between a driver in kernel space and a process in user space (see Figure 2-1).

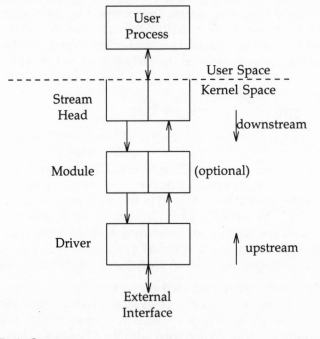

Figure 2-1: Basic Stream

A Stream has three parts: A Stream head, module(s) (optional), and a driver (also referred to as the Stream end). The Stream head provides the interface between the Stream and user processes. Its principal function is to process STREAMS-related user system calls. A module processes data that travel between the Stream head and driver. A STREAMS driver may be a

device driver, providing the services of an external I/O device, or an internal software driver, commonly called a pseudo-device driver.

Using a combination of system calls, kernel routines, and kernel utilities, STREAMS passes data between a driver and the Stream head in the form of messages. Messages that are passed from the Stream head toward the driver are said to travel downstream, and messages passed in the other direction travel upstream.

The Stream head transfers data between the data space of a user process and STREAMS kernel data space. Data sent to a driver from a user process are packaged into STREAMS messages and passed downstream. Messages arriving at the Stream head from downstream are processed by the Stream head, and data are copied into user buffers. STREAMS can insert one or more modules into a Stream between the Stream head and driver to perform intermediate processing of data passing between the Stream head and driver.

System Calls

Applications programmers can use the STREAMS facilities via a set of system calls. This system call interface is upward compatible with the existing character I/O facilities. The **open**(2) system call will recognize a STREAMS file and create a Stream to the specified driver. A user process can send and receive data using **read**(2) and **write**(2) in the same manner as with character files and devices. The **ioctl**(2) system call enables application programs to perform functions specific to a particular device. In addition, a set of generic STREAMS **ioctl** commands [see **streamio**(7)] support a variety of functions for accessing and controlling Streams. A **close**(2) will dismantle a Stream.

open, **close**, **read**, **write**, and **ioctl** support the basic set of operations on Streams. In addition, new system calls support advanced STREAMS facilities. The **poll**(2) system call enables an application program to poll multiple Streams for various events. When used with the STREAMS I_SETSIG **ioctl** command, **poll** allows an application to process I/O in an asynchronous manner. The **putmsg**(2) and **getmsg**(2) system calls enable application programs to interact with STREAMS modules and drivers through a service interface (described next).

These calls are discussed in this document and in the *STREAMS Programmer's Guide*. They are specified in the *Programmer's Reference Manual* and the *System Administrator's Reference Manual*.

Benefits of STREAMS

STREAMS offers two major benefits for applications programmers: easy creation of modules that offer standard data communications services, and the ability to manipulate those modules on a Stream.

Creating Service Interfaces

One benefit of STREAMS is that it simplifies the creation of modules that present a service interface to any neighboring application program, module, or device driver. A service interface is defined at the boundary between two neighbors. In STREAMS, a service interface is a specified set of messages and the rules for allowable sequences of these messages across the boundary. A module that implements a service interface will receive a message from a neighbor and respond with an appropriate action (for example, send back a request to retransmit) based on the specific message received and the preceding sequence of messages.

STREAMS provides features that make it easier to design various application processes and modules to common service interfaces. If these modules are written to comply with industry-standard service interfaces, they are called protocol modules.

In general, any two modules can be connected anywhere in a Stream. However, rational sequences are generally constructed by connecting modules with compatible protocol service interfaces. For example, a module that implements an X.25 protocol layer, as shown in Figure 2-2, presents a protocol service interface at its input and output sides. In this case, other modules should only be connected to the input and output side if they have the compatible X.25 service interface.

Manipulating Modules

STREAMS provides the capabilities to manipulate modules from user level, to interchange modules with common service interfaces, and to present a service interface to a Stream user process. As stated in Chapter 1, these capabilities yield benefits when implementing networking services and protocols, including:

- User level programs can be independent of underlying protocols and physical communication media.

- Network architectures and higher level protocols can be independent of underlying protocols, drivers and physical communication media.

- Higher level services can be created by selecting and connecting lower level services and protocols.

Below are examples of the benefits of STREAMS capabilities to developers for creating service interfaces and manipulating modules.

 NOTE   All protocol modules used below were selected for illustrative purposes. Their use does not imply that AT&T offers such modules as products.

Protocol Portability

Figure 2-2 shows how the same X.25 protocol module can be used with different drivers on different machines by implementing compatible service interfaces. The X.25 protocol module interfaces are Connection Oriented Network Service (CONS) and Link Access Protocol – Balanced (LAPB) driver.

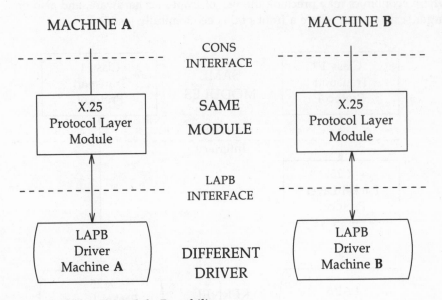

Figure 2-2: Protocol Module Portability

Protocol Substitution

Alternative protocol modules (and device drivers) can be interchanged on the same machine if they are implemented to an equivalent service interface(s).

Protocol Migration

Figure 2-3 illustrates how STREAMS can migrate functions between kernel software and front end firmware. A common downstream service interface allows the transport protocol module to be independent of the number or type of modules below. The same transport module will connect without modification to either an X.25 module or X.25 driver that has the same service interface.

By shifting functions between software and firmware, developers can produce cost effective, functionally equivalent systems over a wide range of configurations. They can rapidly incorporate technological advances. The same transport protocol module can be used on a lower capacity machine,

where economics may preclude the use of front-end hardware, and also on a larger scale system where a front-end is economically justified.

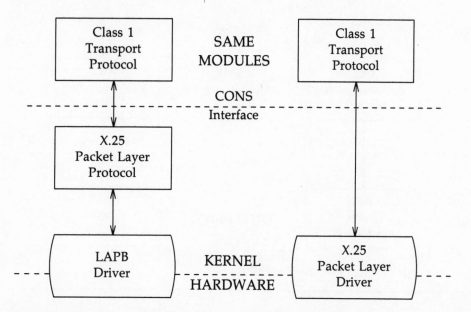

Figure 2-3: Protocol Migration

Module Reusability

Figure 2-4 shows the same canonical module (for example, one that provides delete and kill processing on character strings) reused in two different Streams. This module would typically be implemented as a filter, with no downstream service interface. In both cases, a TTY interface is presented to the Stream's user process since the module is nearest the Stream head.

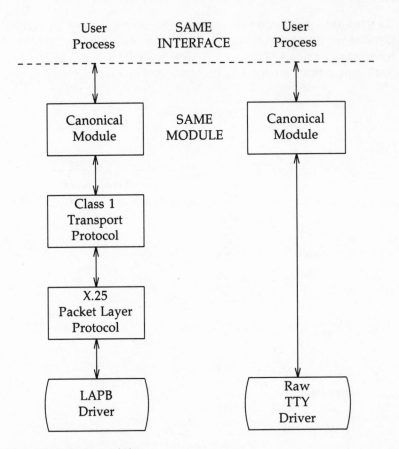

Figure 2-4: Module Reusability

An Advanced View of a Stream

The STREAMS mechanism constructs a Stream by serially connecting kernel resident STREAMS components, each constructed from a specific set of structures. As described earlier and shown in Figure 2-5, the primary STREAMS components are the Stream head, optional module(s), and Stream end.

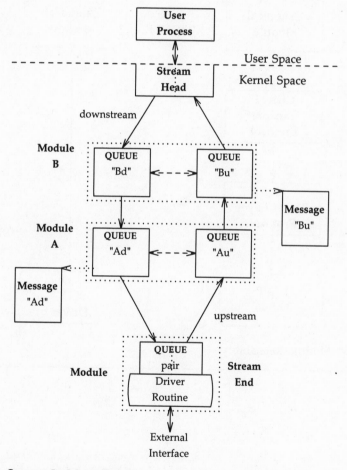

Figure 2-5: Stream In More Detail

Stream Head

The Stream head provides the interface between the Stream and an application program. The Stream head processes STREAMS-related system calls from the application and performs the bidirectional transfer of data and information between the application (in user space) and messages (in STREAMS' kernel space).

Messages are the only means of transferring data and communicating within a Stream. A STREAMS message contains data, status/control information, or a combination of the two. Each message includes a specified message type indicator that identifies the contents.

Modules

A module performs intermediate transformations on messages passing between Stream head and driver. There may be zero or more modules in a Stream (zero when the driver performs all the required character and device processing).

Each module is constructed from a pair of QUEUE structures (see Au/Ad and Bu/Bd in Figure 2-5). A pair is required to implement the bidirectional and symmetrical attributes of a Stream. One QUEUE performs functions on messages passing upstream through the module (Au and Bu in Figure 2-5). The other set (Ad and Bd) performs another set of functions on downstream messages. (A QUEUE, which is part of a module, is different from a message queue, which is described later.)

Each of the two QUEUEs in a module will generally have distinct functions, that is, unrelated processing procedures and data. The QUEUEs operate independently so that Au will not know if a message passes through Ad unless Ad is programmed to inform it. Messages and data can be shared only if the developer specifically programs the module functions to perform the sharing.

Each QUEUE can directly access the adjacent QUEUE in the direction of message flow (for example, Au to Bu or Stream head to Bd). In addition, within a module, a QUEUE can readily locate its mate and access its messages (for example, for echoing) and data.

Each QUEUE in a module may contain or point to messages, processing procedures, or data:

- Messages — These are dynamically attached to the QUEUE on a linked list ("message queue", see Au and Bd in Figure 2-5) as they pass through the module.

- Processing procedures — A put procedure, to process messages, must be incorporated in each QUEUE. An optional service procedure, to share the message processing with the put procedure, can also be incorporated. According to their function, the procedures can send messages upstream and/or downstream, and they can also modify the private data in their module.

- Data — Developers may provide private data if required by the QUEUE to perform message processing (for example, state information and translation tables).

In general, each of the two QUEUEs in a module has a distinct set of all of these elements. Additional module elements will be described later. Although depicted as distinct from modules (see Figure 2-5), a Stream head and the Stream end also contain a pair of QUEUEs.

Stream End

A Stream end is a module in which the module's processing procedures are the driver routines. The procedures in the Stream end are different from those in other modules because they are accessible from an external device and because the STREAMS mechanism allows multiple Streams to be connected to the same driver.

The driver can be a device driver, providing an interface between kernel space and an external communications device, or an internal pseudo-device driver. A pseudo-device driver is not directly related to any external device, and it performs functions internal to the kernel. The multiplexing driver discussed in Chapter 6 is a pseudo-device driver.

Device drivers must transform all data and status/control information between STREAMS message formats and their external representation. Differences between STREAMS and character device drivers are discussed in Chapter 7.

3 BUILDING A STREAM

A Stream is created on the first **open**(2) system call to a character special file corresponding to a STREAMS driver. A STREAMS device is distinguished from other character devices by a field contained in the associated **cdevsw** device table entry.

A Stream is usually built in two steps. Step one creates a minimal Stream consisting of just the Stream head and device driver, and step two adds modules to produce an expanded Stream (see Figure 3-1). The first step has three parts: head and driver structures are allocated and initialized; the modules in the head and end are linked to each other to form a Stream; the driver open routine is called.

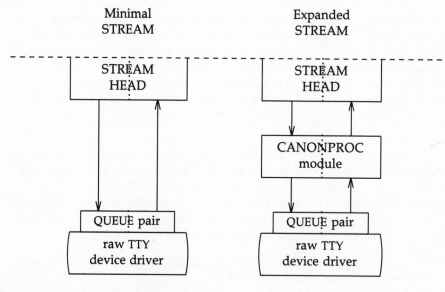

Figure 3-1: Setting Up a Stream

If the driver performs all character and device processing required, no modules need be added to a Stream. Examples of STREAMS drivers include a raw tty driver (one that passes along input characters without change) and a driver with multiple Streams open to it (corresponding to multiple minor devices opened to a character device driver).

When the driver receives characters from the device, it places them into messages. The messages are then transferred to the next Stream component, the Stream head, which extracts the contents of the message and copies them to user space. Similar processing occurs for downstream character output; the Stream head copies data from user space into messages and sends them to the driver.

Expanded Streams

As the second step in building a Stream, modules can be added to the Stream. In the right-hand Stream in Figure 3-1, the CANONPROC module was added to provide additional processing on the characters sent between head and driver.

Modules are added and removed from a Stream in last-in-first-out (LIFO) order. They are inserted and deleted at the Stream head via the **ioctl**(2) system call. In the Stream on the left of Figure 2-4, the X.25 module was the first added to the Stream, followed by Class 1 Transport and Canonical modules. To replace the Class 1 module with a Class 0 module, the Canonical module would have to be removed first, then the Class 1 module, then a Class 0 module would be added and the Canonical module put back.

Because adding and removing modules resembles stack operations, the add is called a push and the remove a pop. Push and pop are two of the **ioctl** functions included in the STREAMS subset of **ioctl** system calls. These commands perform various manipulations and operations on Streams. The modules manipulated in this manner are called pushable modules, in contrast to the modules contained in the Stream head and end. This stack terminology applies only to the setup, modification, and breakdown of a Stream.

> NOTE | Subsequent use of the word module will refer to those pushable modules between Stream head and end.

The Stream head processes the **ioctl** and executes the push, which is analogous to opening the Stream driver. Modules are referenced by a unique symbolic name, contained in the STREAMS **fmodsw** module table (similar to the **cdevsw** table associated with a device file). The module table and module name are internal to STREAMS and are accessible from user space only through STREAMS **ioctl** system calls. The **fmodsw** table points to the module template in the kernel. When a module is pushed, the template is located, the

module structures for both QUEUES are allocated, and the template values are copied into the structures.

In addition to the module elements described in "A Basic View of a Stream" section of Chapter 2, each module contains pointers to an open routine and a close routine. The open is called when the module is pushed, and the close is called when the module is popped. Module open and close procedures are similar to a driver open and close.

As in other files, a STREAMS file is closed when the last process open to it closes the file by a **close**(2) system call. This system call causes the Stream to be dismantled (modules popped and the driver close executed).

Pushable Modules

Modules are pushed onto a Stream to provide special functions and/or additional protocol layers. In Figure 3-1, the Stream on the left is opened in a minimal configuration with a raw tty driver and no other module added. The driver receives one character at a time from the device, places the character in a message, and sends the message upstream. The Stream head receives the message, extracts the single character, and copies it into the reading process buffer to send to the user process in response to a **read**(2) system call. When the user process wants to send characters back to the driver, it issues a **write**(2) system call, and the characters are sent to the Stream head. The head copies the characters into one or more multi-character messages and sends them downstream. An application program requiring no further kernel character processing would use this minimal Stream.

A user requiring a more terminal-like interface would need to insert a module to perform functions such as echoing, character-erase, and line-kill. Assuming that the CANONPROC module in Figure 3-1 fulfills this need, the application program first opens a raw tty Stream. Then, the CANONPROC module is pushed above the driver to create a Stream of the form shown on the right of the figure. The driver is not aware that a module has been placed above it and therefore continues to send single character messages upstream. The module receives single character messages from the driver, processes the characters, and accumulates them into line strings. Each line is placed into a message and sent to the Stream head. The head now finds more than one character in the messages it receives from downstream.

Stream head implementation accommodates this change in format automatically and transfers the multiple-character data into user space. The Stream head also keeps track of messages partially transferred into user space (for example, when the current user **read** buffer can only hold part of the current message). Downstream operation is not affected: the head sends, and the driver receives, multiple character messages.

Note that the Stream head provides the interface between the Stream and user process. Modules and drivers do not have to implement user interface functions other than open and close.

4 USER LEVEL FUNCTIONS

STREAMS System Calls

After a Stream has been opened, STREAMS-related system calls allow a
user process to insert and delete (push and pop) modules. That process can
then communicate with and control the operation of the Stream head,
modules, and drivers, and can send and receive messages containing data and
control information. This chapter presents an example of some of the basic
functions available to STREAMS-based applications via the system calls. Additional functions are described at the end of this chapter and in Chapter 6.

The full set of STREAMS-related system calls is:

open(2)   Open a Stream (described in Chapter 3)

close(2)   Close a Stream (described in Chapter 3)

read(2)   Read data from a Stream

write(2)   Write data to a Stream

ioctl(2)   Control a Stream

getmsg(2)   Receive the message at Stream head

putmsg(2)   Send a message downstream

poll(2)   Notify the application program when selected events occur
             on a Stream

The following two-part example describes a Stream that controls the data
communication characteristics of a connection between an asynchronous terminal and a tty port. It illustrates basic user level STREAMS features, then
shows how messages can be used. Chapter 5 discusses the kernel level
Stream operations corresponding to the user level operations described in this
chapter. See the *STREAMS Programmer's Guide* for more detailed examples of
STREAMS applications, modules, and drivers.

An Asynchronous Protocol Stream Example

In the example, our computer runs the UNIX system and supports different kinds of asynchronous terminals, each logging in on its own port. The port hardware is limited in function; for example, it detects and reports line and modem status, but does not check parity.

Communications software support for these terminals is provided via a STREAMS implemented asynchronous protocol. The protocol includes a variety of options that are set when a terminal operator dials in to log on. The options are determined by a **getty**-type STREAMS user process, *getstrm*, which analyzes data sent to it through a series of dialogs (prompts and responses) between the process and terminal operator.

The process sets the terminal options for the duration of the connection by pushing modules onto the Stream or by sending control messages to cause changes in modules (or in the device driver) already on the Stream. The options supported include:

- ASCII or EBCDIC character codes

- For ASCII code, the parity (odd, even or none)

- Echo or not echo input characters

- Canonical input and output processing or transparent (raw) character handling

These options are set with the following modules:

CHARPROC   Provides input character processing functions, including dynamically settable (via control messages passed to the module) character echo and parity checking. The module's default settings are to echo characters and not check character parity.

CANONPROC   Performs canonical processing on ASCII characters upstream and downstream (note that this performs some processing in a different manner from the standard UNIX system character I/O tty subsystem).

ASCEBC   Translates EBCDIC code to ASCII upstream and ASCII to EBCDIC downstream.

Initializing the Stream

At system initialization a user process, *getstrm*, is created for each tty port. *getstrm* opens a Stream to its port and pushes the CHARPROC module onto the Stream by use of an **ioctl** I_PUSH command. Then, the process issues a **getmsg** system call to the Stream and sleeps until a message reaches the Stream head. The Stream is now in its idle state.

The initial idle Stream, shown in Figure 4-1, contains only one pushable module, CHARPROC. The device driver is a limited function raw tty driver connected to a limited-function communication port. The driver and port transparently transmit and receive one unbuffered character at a time.

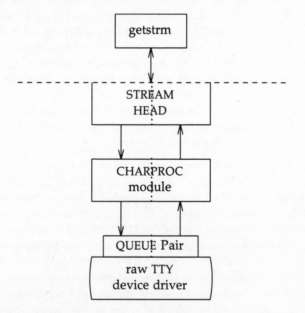

Figure 4-1: Idle Stream Configuration for Example

Upon receipt of initial input from a tty port, *getstrm* establishes a connection with the terminal, analyzes the option requests, verifies them, and issues STREAMS system calls to set the options. After setting up the options, *getstrm* creates a user application process. Later, when the user terminates that application, *getstrm* restores the Stream to its idle state by use of system calls.

The next step is to analyze in more detail how the Stream sets up the communications options. Before doing so, let's examine how messages are handled in STREAMS.

Message Types

All STREAMS messages are assigned message types to indicate their intended use by modules and drivers and to determine their handling by the Stream head. A driver or module can assign most types to a message it generates, and a module can modify a message's type during processing. The Stream head will convert certain system calls to specified message types and send them downstream, and it will respond to other calls by copying the contents of certain message types that were sent upstream. Messages exist only in the kernel, so a user process can only send and receive buffers. The process is not explicitly aware of the message type, but it may be aware of message boundaries, depending on the system call used (see the distinction between **getmsg** and **read** in the next section).

Most message types are internal to STREAMS and can only be passed from one STREAMS module to another. A few message types, including M_DATA, M_PROTO, and M_PCPROTO, can also be passed between a Stream and user processes. M_DATA messages carry data within a Stream and between a Stream and a user process. M_PROTO or M_PCPROTO messages carry both data and control information. However, the distinction between control information and data is generally determined by the developer when implementing a particular Stream. Control information includes service interface information, carried between two Stream entities that present service interfaces, and condition or status information, which may be sent between any two Stream entities regardless of their interface. An M_PCPROTO message has the same general use as an M_PROTO, but the former moves faster through a Stream (see "Message Queue Priority" in Chapter 6).

Sending and Receiving Messages

putmsg is a STREAMS-related system call that sends messages; it is similar to **write**. **putmsg** provides a data buffer which is converted into an M_DATA message, and can also provide a separate control buffer to be placed into an M_PROTO or M_PCPROTO block. **write** provides byte-stream data to be converted into M_DATA messages.

getmsg is a STREAMS-related system call that accepts messages; it is similar to **read**. One difference between the two calls is that **read** accepts only data (messages sent upstream to the Stream head as message type M_DATA), such as the characters entered from the terminal. **getmsg** can simultaneously accept both data and control information (message sent upstream as types M_PROTO or M_PCPROTO). **getmsg** also differs from **read** in that it preserves message boundaries so that the same boundaries exist above and below the Stream head (that is, between a user process and a Stream). **read** generally ignores message boundaries, processing data as a byte stream.

Certain STREAMS **ioctl** commands, such as I_STR, also cause messages to be sent or received on the Stream. I_STR provides the general "ioctl" capability of the character I/O subsystem. A user process above the Stream head can issue **putmsg**, **getmsg**, the I_STR **ioctl** command, and certain other STREAMS related system calls. Other STREAMS **ioctl**s perform functions that include changing the state of the Stream head, pushing and popping modules, or returning special information. **ioctl** commands are described in more detail the *STREAMS Programmer's Guide*.

In addition to message types that explicitly transfer data to a process, some messages sent upstream result in information transfer. When these messages reach the Stream head, they are transformed into various forms and sent to the user process. The forms include signals, error codes, and call return values.

Using Messages in the Example

Returning to the asynchronous protocol example, the Stream was in its idle configuration (see Figure 4-1). *getstrm* had issued a **getmsg** and was sleeping until the arrival of a message from the Stream head. Such a message would result from the driver detecting activity on the associated tty port.

An incoming call arrives at port one and causes a ring detect signal in the modem. The driver receives the ring signal, answers the call, and sends upstream an M_PROTO message containing information indicating an incoming call. *getstrm* is notified of all incoming calls, although it can choose to refuse the call because of system limits. In this idle state, *getstrm* will also accept M_PROTO messages indicating, for example, error conditions such as detection of line or modem problems on the idle line.

The M_PROTO message containing notification of the incoming call flows upstream from the driver into CHARPROC. CHARPROC inspects the message type, determines that message processing is not required, and passes the unmodified message upstream to the Stream head. The Stream head copies the message into the **getmsg** buffers (one buffer for control information, the other for data) associated with *getstrm* and wakes up the process. *getstrm* sends its acceptance of the incoming call with a **putmsg** system call which results in a downstream M_PROTO message to the driver.

Then, *getstrm* sends a prompt to the operator with a **write** and issues a **getmsg** to receive the response. A **read** could have been used to receive the response, but the **getmsg** call allows concurrent monitoring for control (M_PROTO and M_PCPROTO) information. *getstrm* will now sleep until the response characters, or information regarding possible error conditions detected by modules or driver, are sent upstream.

The first response, sent upstream in a M_DATA block, indicates that the code set is ASCII and that canonical processing is requested. *getstrm* implements these options by pushing CANONPROC onto the Stream, above CHAR-PROC, to perform canonical processing on the input ASCII characters.

The response to the next prompt requests even parity checking. *getstrm* sends an **ioctl** I_STR command to CHARPROC, requesting the module to perform even parity checking on upstream characters. When the dialog indicate protocol option setting is complete, *getstrm* creates an application process. At the end of the connection, *getstrm* will pop CANONPROC and then send a I_STR to CHARPROC requesting the module to restore the no-parity idle state (CHARPROC remains on the Stream).

As a result of the above dialogs, the terminal at port one operates in the following configuration:

- ASCII, even parity

- Echo

- Canonical processing

In similar fashion, an operator at a different type of terminal on port two requests a different set of options, resulting in the following configuration:

- EBCDIC

- No Echo

- Canonical processing

The resultant Streams for the two ports are shown in Figure 4-2. For port one, on the left, the modules in the Stream are CANONPROC and CHARPROC.

For port two, on the right, the resultant modules are CANONPROC, ASCEBC and CHARPROC. ASCEBC has been pushed on this Stream to translate between the ASCII interface at the downstream side of CANONPROC and the EBCDIC interface of the upstream output side of CHARPROC. In addition, *getstrm* has sent an I_STR to the CHARPROC module in this Stream requesting it to disable echo. The resultant modification to CHARPROC's functions is indicated by the word "modified" in the right Stream of Figure 4-2.

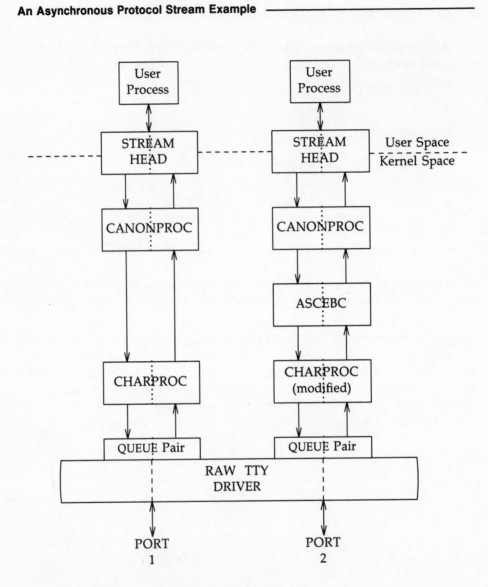

Figure 4-2: Asynchronous Terminal Streams

Since CHARPROC is now performing no function for port two, it might have been popped from the Stream to be reinserted by *getstrm* at the end of connection. However, the low overhead of STREAMS does not require its removal. The module remains on the Stream, passing messages unmodified between ASCEBC and the driver. At the end of the connection, *getstrm* restores this Stream to its idle configuration of Figure 4-1 by popping the added modules and then sending an I_STR to CHARPROC to restore the echo default.

Note that the tty driver shown in Figure 4-2 handles minor devices. Each minor device has a distinct Stream connected from user space to the driver. This ability to handle multiple devices is a standard STREAMS feature, similar to the minor device mechanism in character I/O device drivers.

Other User Functions

The previous example illustrates basic STREAMS concepts. Alternate, more efficient, STREAMS calls or mechanisms could have been used in place of those described earlier. Some of the alternatives are described in Chapter 6 and others are addressed in the *STREAMS Programmer's Guide*.

For example, the initialization process that created a *getstrm* for each tty port could have been implemented as a "supergetty" by use of the STREAMS-related **poll** system call. As described in Chapter 6, **poll** allows a single process to efficiently monitor and control multiple Streams. The "supergetty" process would handle all of the Stream and terminal protocol initialization and would create application processes only for established connections.

The M_PROTO notification sent to *getstrm* could have been sent by the driver as an M_SIG message that causes a specified signal to be sent to the process. As discussed previously under "Message Types," error and status information can also be sent upstream from a driver or module to user processes via different message types. These messages will be transformed by the Stream head into a signal or error code.

Finally, an **ioctl** I_STR command could have been used in place of a **putmsg** M_PROTO message to send information to a driver. The sending process must receive an explicit response from an I_STR by a specified time period or an error will be returned. A response message must be sent upstream by the destination module or driver to be translated into the user response by the Stream head.

5   KERNEL LEVEL FUNCTIONS

Introduction

This chapter introduces the use of the STREAMS mechanism in the kernel and describes some of the tools provided by STREAMS to assist in the development of modules and drivers. In addition to the basic message passing mechanism and QUEUE Stream linkage described previously, the STREAMS mechanism consists of various facilities including buffer management, the STREAMS scheduler, processing and message priority, flow control, and multiplexing. Over 30 STREAMS utility routines and macros are available to manipulate and utilize these facilities.

The key elements of a STREAMS kernel implementation are the processing routines in the module and drivers, and the preparation of required data structures. The structures are described in the *STREAMS Programmer's Guide*. The following sections provide further information on messages and on the processing routines that operate on them. The example of Chapter 4 is continued, associating the user-level operations described there with kernel operations.

Messages

As shown in Figure 5-1, a STREAMS message consists of one or more linked message blocks. That is, the first message block of a message may be attached to other message blocks that are part of the same message. Multiple blocks in a message can occur, for example, as the result of processing that adds header or trailer data to the data contained in the message, or because of message buffer size limitations which cause the data to span multiple blocks. When a message is composed of multiple message blocks, the message type of the first block determines the type of the entire message, regardless of the types of the attached message blocks.

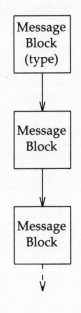

Figure 5-1: A Message

STREAMS allocates a message as a single block containing a buffer of a certain size (see the next section). If the data for a message exceed the size of the buffer containing the data, the procedure can allocate a new block containing a larger buffer, copy the current data to it, insert the new data and deallocate the old block. Alternately, the procedure can allocate an additional

(smaller) block, place the new data in the new message block and link it after or before the initial message block. Both alternatives yield one new message.

Messages can exist standalone, as shown in Figure 5-1, when the message is being processed by a procedure. Alternately, a message can await processing on a linked list of messages, called a message queue, in a QUEUE. In Figure 5-2, Message 1 is linked to Message 2.

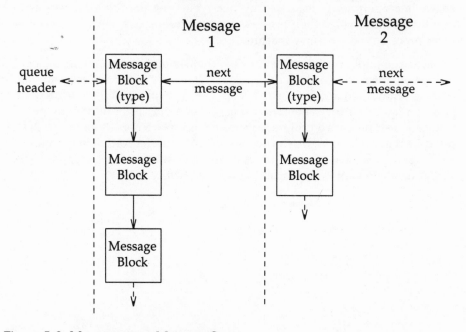

Figure 5-2: Messages on a Message Queue

When a message is on a queue, the first block of the message contains links to preceding and succeeding messages on the same message queue, in addition to containing a link to the second block of the message (if present). The message queue head and tail are contained in the QUEUE.

STREAMS utility routines enable developers to manipulate messages and message queues.

Message Allocation

STREAMS maintains its own storage pool for messages. A procedure can request the allocation of a message of a specified size at one of three message pool priorities. The **allocb** utility will return a message containing a single block with a buffer of at least the size requested, providing there is a buffer available at the priority requested. When requesting priority for messages, developers must weigh their process' need for resources against the needs of other processes on the same machine.

Message pool priority generally has no effect on allocation until the pool falls below internal STREAMS thresholds. When this occurs, **allocb** may refuse a lower priority request for a message of size "x" while granting a higher priority request for the same size message. As examples of priority usage, storage for an urgent control message, such as an M_HANGUP or M_PCPROTO could be requested at high priority. An M_DATA buffer for holding input might be requested at medium priority, and an output buffer (presuming the output data can wait in user space) at lowest priority.

Put and Service Procedures

The procedures in the QUEUE are the software routines that process messages as they transit the QUEUE. The processing is generally performed according to the message type and can result in a modified message, new message(s) or no message. A resultant message is generally sent in the same direction in which it was received by the QUEUE, but may be sent in either direction. A QUEUE will always contain a put procedure and may also contain an associated service procedure.

Put Procedures

A put procedure is the QUEUE routine that receives messages from the preceding QUEUE in the Stream. Messages are passed between QUEUEs by a procedure in one QUEUE calling the put procedure contained in the following QUEUE. A call to the put procedure in the appropriate direction is generally the only way to pass messages between modules (unless otherwise indicated, "modules" infers "module, driver and Stream head"). QUEUEs in pushable (see Chapter 3) modules contain a put procedure. In general, there is a separate put procedure for the read and write QUEUEs in a module because of the "full duplex" operation of most Streams.

A put procedure is associated with immediate (as opposed to deferred, see below) processing on a message. Each module accesses the adjacent put procedure as a subroutine. For example, consider that *modA*, *modB*, and *modC* are three consecutive modules in a Stream, with *modC* connected to the Stream head. If *modA* receives a message to be sent upstream, *modA* processes that message and calls *modB*'s put procedure, which processes it and calls *modC*'s put procedure, which processes it and calls the Stream head's put procedure. Thus, the message will be passed along the Stream in one continuous processing sequence. On one hand, this sequence has the benefit of completing the entire processing in a short time with low overhead (subroutine calls). On the other hand, if this sequence is lengthy and the processing is implemented on a multi-user system, then this manner of processing may be good for this Stream but may be detrimental for others since they may have to wait "too long" to get their turn at bat.

In addition, there are situations where the put procedure cannot immediately process the message but must hold it until processing is allowed. The most typical examples of this are a driver which must wait until the current

output completes before sending the next message and the Stream head, which may have to wait until a process initiates a **read**(2) on the Stream.

Service Procedures

STREAMS allows a service procedure to be contained in each QUEUE, in addition to the put procedure, to address the above cases and for additional purposes. A service procedure is not required in a QUEUE and is associated with deferred processing. If a QUEUE has both a put and service procedure, message processing will generally be divided between the procedures. The put procedure is always called first, from a preceding QUEUE. After the put procedure completes its part of the message processing, it arranges for the service procedure to be called by passing the message to the **putq** routine. **putq** does two things: it places the message on the message queue of the QUEUE (see Figure 5-2) and links the QUEUE to the end of the STREAMS scheduling queue. When **putq** returns to the put procedure, the procedure typically exits. Some time later, the service procedure will be automatically called by the STREAMS scheduler.

The STREAMS scheduler is separate and distinct from the UNIX system process scheduler. It is concerned only with QUEUEs linked on the STREAMS scheduling queue. The scheduler calls the service procedure of the scheduled QUEUE in a FIFO manner, one at a time.

Having both a put and service procedure in a QUEUE enables STREAMS to provide the rapid response and the queuing required in multi-user systems. The put procedure allows rapid response to certain data and events, such as software echoing of input characters. Put procedures effectively have higher priority than any scheduled service procedures. When called from the preceding STREAMS component, a put procedure executes before the scheduled service procedures of any QUEUE are executed.

The service procedure implies message queuing. Queuing results in deferred processing of the service procedure, following all other QUEUEs currently on the scheduling queue. For example, terminal output and input erase and kill processing would typically be performed in a service procedure because this type of processing does not have to be as timely as echoing. Use of a service procedure also allows processing time to be more evenly spread among multiple Streams. As with the put procedure there will generally be a separate service procedure for each QUEUE in a module. The flow control mechanism (see Chapter 6) uses the service procedures.

Kernel Processing

The following continues the example of Chapter 4, describing STREAMS kernel operations and associates them, where relevant, with Chapter 4 user-level system calls in the example. As a result of initializing operations and pushing a module, the Stream for port one has the following configuration:

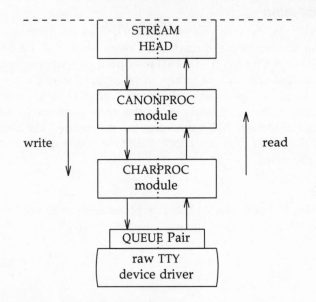

Figure 5-3: Operational Stream for Example

As shown in Figure 5-3, the upstream QUEUE is also referred to as the read QUEUE, reflecting the message flow in response to a **read** system call. Correspondingly, downstream is referred to as the write QUEUE. Read side processing is discussed first.

Read Side Processing

In our example, read side processing consists of driver processing, CHARPROC processing, and CANONPROC processing.

Driver Processing

In the example, the user process has blocked on the **getmsg**(2) system call while waiting for a message to reach the Stream head, and the device driver independently waits for input of a character from the port hardware or for a message from upstream. Upon receipt of an input character interrupt from the port, the driver places the associated character in an M_DATA message, allocated previously. Then, the driver sends the message to the CHARPROC module by calling CHARPROC's upstream put procedure. On return from CHARPROC, the driver calls the **allocb** utility routine to get another message for the next character.

CHARPROC

CHARPROC has both put and service procedures on its read side. In the example, the other QUEUEs in the modules also have put and service procedures:

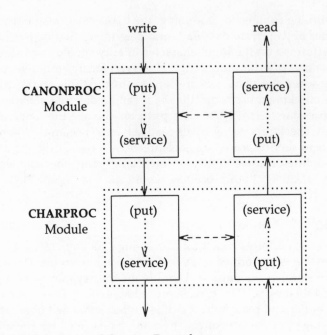

Figure 5-4: Module Put and Service Procedures

When the driver calls CHARPROC's read QUEUE put procedure, the procedure checks private data flags in the QUEUE. In this case, the flags indicate that echoing is to be performed (recall that echoing is optional and that we are working with port hardware which can not automatically echo). CHARPROC causes the echo to be transmitted back to the terminal by first making a copy of the message with a STREAMS utility. Then, CHARPROC uses another utility to obtain the address of its own write QUEUE. Finally, the CHARPROC read put procedure calls its write put procedure and passes it the message copy. The write procedure sends the message to the driver to effect the echo and then returns to the read procedure.

This part of read side processing is implemented with put procedures so that the entire processing sequence occurs as an extension of the driver input character interrupt. The CHARPROC read and write put procedures appear as subroutines (nested in the case of the write procedure) to the driver. This manner of processing is intended to produce the character echo in a minimal time frame.

After returning from echo processing, the CHARPROC read put procedure checks another of its private data flags and determines that parity checking should be performed on the input character. Parity should most reasonably be checked as part of echo processing. However, for this example, parity is checked only when the characters are sent upstream. This relaxes the timing in which the checking must occur, that is, it can be deferred along with the canonical processing. CHARPROC uses **putq** to schedule the (original) message for parity check processing by its read service procedure. When the CHARPROC read service procedure is complete, it forwards the message to the read put procedure of CANONPROC. Note that if parity checking were not required, the CHARPROC put procedure would call the CANONPROC put procedure directly.

CANONPROC

CANONPROC performs canonical processing. As implemented, all read QUEUE processing is performed in its service procedure so that CANONPROC's put procedure simply calls **putq** to schedule the message for its read service procedure and then exits. The service procedure extracts the character from the message buffer and place it in the "line buffer" contained in another M_DATA message it is constructing. Then, the message which contained the single character is returned to the buffer pool. If the character received was not an end-of-line, CANONPROC exits. Otherwise, a complete line has been assembled and CANONPROC sends the message upstream to the Stream head which unblocks the user process from the **getmsg** call and passes it the contents of the message.

Write Side Processing

The write side of this Stream carries two kinds of messages from the user process: **ioctl** messages for CHARPROC, and M_DATA messages to be output to the terminal.

ioctl messages are sent downstream as a result of an I_STR **ioctl** system call. When CHARPROC receives an **ioctl** message type, it processes the message contents to modify internal QUEUE flags and then uses a utility to send an acknowledgement message upstream (read side) to the Stream head. The Stream head acts on the acknowledgement message by unblocking the user from the **ioctl**.

For terminal output, it is presumed that M_DATA messages, sent by **write** system calls, contain multiple characters. In general, STREAMS returns to the user process immediately after processing the **write** call so that the process may send additional messages. Flow control, described in the next chapter, will eventually block the sending process. The messages can queue on the write side of the driver because of character transmission timing. When a message is received by the driver's write put procedure, the procedure will use **putq** to place the message on its write-side service message queue if the driver is currently transmitting a previous message buffer. However, there is generally no write QUEUE service procedure in a device driver. Driver output interrupt processing takes the place of scheduling and performs the service procedure functions, removing messages from the queue.

Analysis

For reasons of efficiency, a module implementation would generally avoid placing one character per message and using separate routines to echo and parity check each character, as was done in this example. Nevertheless, even this design yields potential benefits. Consider a case where alternate, more intelligent port hardware was substituted. If the hardware processed multiple input characters and performed the echo and parity checking functions of CHARPROC, then the new driver could be implemented to present the same interface as CHARPROC. Other modules such as CANONPROC could continue to be used without modification.

6 OTHER FACILITIES

Introduction

The previous chapters described the basic concepts of constructing a Stream and utilizing the STREAMS mechanism. Additional STREAMS features are provided to handle characteristic problems of protocol implementation, such as flow control, and to assist in development.

There are also kernel and user-level facilities that support the implementation of advanced functions, such as multiplexors, and allow asynchronous operation of a user process and STREAMS input and output.

Message Queue Priority

As mentioned in the previous chapter, the STREAMS scheduler operates strictly FIFO so that each QUEUE's service procedure receives control in the order it was scheduled. When a service procedure receives control, it may encounter multiple messages on its message queue. This buildup can occur if there is a long interval between the time a message is queued by a put procedure and the time that the STREAMS scheduler calls the associated service procedure. In this interval, there can be multiple calls to the put procedure causing multiple messages. The service procedure always processes all messages on its message queue unless prevented by flow control (see next section). Each message must pass through all the modules connecting its origin and destination in the Stream.

If service procedures were used in all QUEUES and there was no message priority, then the most recently scheduled message would be processed after all the other scheduled messages on all Streams had been processed. In certain cases, message types containing urgent information (such as a break or alarm conditions) must pass through the Stream quickly. To accommodate these cases, STREAMS provides two classes of message queuing priority, ordinary and high. STREAMS prevents high-priority messages from being blocked by flow control and causes a service procedure to process them ahead of all ordinary priority messages on the procedure's queue. This results in the high-priority message transiting each module with minimal delay.

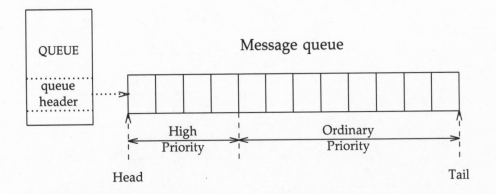

Figure 6-1: Streams Message Priority

The priority mechanism operates as shown in Figure 6-1. Message queues are generally not present in a QUEUE unless that QUEUE contains a service procedure. When a message is passed to **putq** to schedule the message for service procedure processing, **putq** places the message on the message queue in priority order. High priority messages are placed ahead of all ordinary priority messages, but behind any other high priority messages on the queue. STREAMS utilities deliver the messages to the processing service procedure FIFO within each priority class. The service procedure is unaware of the message priority and simply receives the next message.

Message priority is defined by the message type; once a message is created, its priority cannot be changed. Certain message types come in equivalent high/ordinary priority pairs (for example, M_PCPROTO and M_PROTO), so that a module or device driver can choose between the two priorities when sending information.

Flow Control

Even on a well-designed system, general system delays, malfunctions, and excessive message accumulation on one or more Streams can cause the message buffer pools to become depleted. Additionally, processing bursts can arise when a service procedure in one module has a long message queue and processes all its messages in one pass. STREAMS provides two independent mechanisms to guard its message buffer pools from being depleted and to minimize long processing bursts at any one module.

NOTE
Flow control is only applied to normal priority messages (see previous section) and not to high priority messages.

The first flow control mechanism is global and automatic and is related to the message pool priority, discussed in the "Message Storage Pool" section of Chapter 5. When the Stream head requests a message buffer in response to a **putmsg** or **write** system call, it uses the lowest level of priority. Since buffer availability is based on priority and buffer pool levels, the Stream head will be among the first modules refused a buffer when the pool becomes depleted. In response, the Stream head will block user output until the STREAMS buffer pool recovers. As a result, output has a lower priority than input.

The second flow control mechanism is local to each Stream and advisory (voluntary), and limits the number of characters that can be queued for processing at any QUEUE in a Stream. This mechanism limits the buffers and related processing at any one QUEUE and in any one Stream, but does not consider buffer pool levels or buffer usage in other Streams.

The advisory mechanism operates between the two nearest QUEUEs in a Stream containing service procedures (see diagram on next page). Messages are generally held on a message queue only if a service procedure is present in the associated QUEUE.

Messages accumulate at a QUEUE when its service procedure processing does not keep pace with the message arrival rate, or when the procedure is blocked from placing its messages on the following Stream component by the flow control mechanism. Pushable modules contain independent upstream and downstream limits, which are set when a developer specifies high-water and low-water control values for the QUEUE. The Stream head contains a preset upstream limit (which can be modified by a special message sent from downstream) and a driver may contain a downstream limit.

Flow control operates as follows:

1. Each time a STREAMS message handling routine (for example, **putq**) adds or removes a message from a message queue in a QUEUE, the limits are checked. STREAMS calculates the total size of all message blocks on the message queue.

2. The total is compared to the QUEUE high-water and low-water values. If the total exceeds the high-water value, an internal full indicator is set for the QUEUE. The operation of the service procedure in this QUEUE is not affected if the indicator is set, and the service procedure continues to be scheduled.

3. The next part of flow control processing occurs in the nearest preceding QUEUE that contains a service procedure. In the diagram below, if D is full and C has no service procedure, then B is the nearest preceding QUEUE.

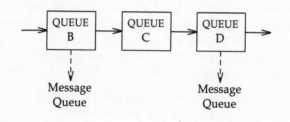

Figure 6-2: Flow Control

4. The service procedure in B uses a STREAMS utility routine to see if a QUEUE ahead is marked full. If messages cannot be sent, the scheduler blocks the service procedure in B from further execution. B remains blocked until the low-water mark of the full QUEUE, D, is reached.

5. While B is blocked, any non-priority messages that arrive at B will accumulate on its message queue (recall that priority messages are not blocked). In turn, B can reach a full state and the full condition will propagate back to the last module in the Stream.

6. When the service procedure processing on D causes the message block total to fall below the low water mark, the full indicator is turned off. Then, STREAMS automatically schedules the nearest preceding blocked QUEUE (B in this case), getting things moving again. This automatic scheduling is know as back-enabling a QUEUE.

Note that to utilize flow control, a developer need only call the utility that tests if a full condition exists ahead, plus perform some housekeeping if it does. Everything else is automatically handled by STREAMS. Additional flow control features are described in the *STREAMS Programmer's Guide*.

Multiplexing

STREAMS multiplexing supports the development of internetworking protocols such as IP and ISO CLNS, and the processing of interleaved data streams such as in SNA, X.25, and terminal window facilities.

STREAMS multiplexors (also called pseudo-device drivers) are created in the kernel by interconnecting multiple Streams. Conceptually, there are two kinds of multiplexors that developers can build with STREAMS: upper and lower multiplexors. Lower multiplexors have multiple lower Streams between device drivers and the multiplexor, and upper multiplexors have multiple upper Streams between user processes the multiplexor.

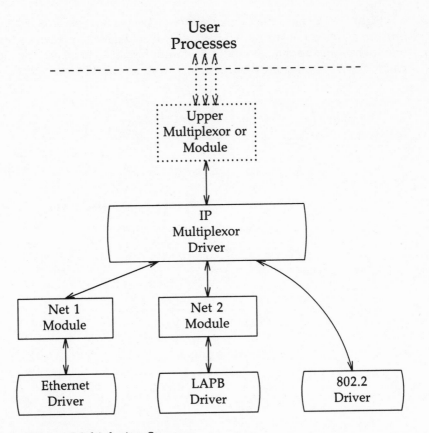

Figure 6-3: Internet Multiplexing Stream

Figure 6-3 shows an example of a lower multiplexor. This configuration would typically occur where internetworking functions were included in the system. This Stream contains two types of drivers: the Ethernet, LAPB, and IEEE 802.2 are hardware device drivers that terminate links to other nodes; the IP (Internet Protocol) is a multiplexor.

The IP multiplexor switches messages among the various nodes (lower Streams) or sends them upstream to user processes in the system. In this example, the multiplexor expects to see an 802.2 interface downstream; for the Ethernet and LAPB drivers, the Net 1 and Net 2 modules provide service interfaces to the two the non-802.2 drivers and the IP multiplexor.

Figure 6-3 depicts the IP multiplexor as part of a larger Stream. The Stream, as shown in the dotted rectangle, would generally have an upper TCP multiplexor and additional modules. Multiplexors could also be cascaded below the IP driver if the device drivers were replaced by multiplexor drivers.

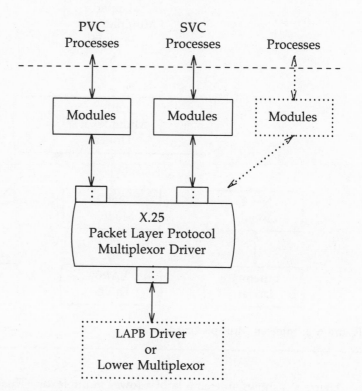

Figure 6-4: X.25 Multiplexing Stream

Figure 6-4 shows an upper multiplexor. In this configuration, the driver routes messages between the lower Stream and one of the upper Streams. This Stream performs X.25 multiplexing to multiple independent SVC (Switched Virtual Circuit) and PVC (Permanent Virtual Circuit) user processes. Upper multiplexors are a specific application of standard STREAMS facilities that support multiple minor devices in a device driver. This figure also shows that more complex configurations can be built by having one or more multiplexed LAPB drivers below and multiple modules above.

Developers can choose either upper or lower multiplexing, or both, when designing their applications. For example, a window multiplexor would have a similar configuration to the X.25 configuration of Figure 6-4, with a window driver replacing Packet Layer, a tty driver replacing LAPB, and the child processes of the terminal process replacing the user processes. Although the X.25 and window multiplexing Streams have similar configurations, their multiplexor drivers would differ significantly. The IP multiplexor of Figure 6-2 has a different configuration than the X.25 multiplexor and the driver would implement its own set of processing and routing requirements.

In addition to upper and lower multiplexors, more complex configurations can be created by connecting Streams containing multiplexors to other multiplexor drivers. With such a diversity of needs for multiplexors, it is not possible to provide general purpose multiplexor drivers. Rather, STREAMS provides a general purpose multiplexing facility. The facility allows users to set up the inter-module/driver plumbing to create multiplexor configurations of generally unlimited interconnection.

The connections are created from user space through specific STREAMS **ioctl** system calls. In a lower multiplexor, multiple Streams are connected below an application-specific, developer-implemented multiplexing driver. The multiplexing facility will only connect Streams to a driver. The **ioctl** call configures a multiplexor by connecting one Stream at a time below the opened multiplexor driver. As each Stream is connected to the driver, the connection setup procedure identifies the Stream to the driver. The driver will generally store this setup information in a private data structure for later use.

Subsequently, when messages flow into the driver on the various connected Streams, the identity of the associated Stream is passed to the driver as part of the standard procedure call. The driver then has available the Stream identification, the previously stored setup information for this Stream, and any internal routing information contained in the message. These data are used, according to the application implemented, to process the incoming message and route the output to the appropriate outgoing Stream.

Additionally, new Streams can be dynamically connected to an operating multiplexor without interfering with ongoing traffic, and existing Streams can be disconnected with similar ease.

Monitoring

STREAMS allows user processes to monitor and control Streams so that system resources (such as CPU cycles and process slots) can be used effectively. Monitoring is especially useful to user-level multiplexors, in which a user process can create multiple Streams and switch messages among them (similar to STREAMS kernel-level multiplexing, described previously).

User processes can efficiently monitor and control multiple Streams with two STREAMS system calls: **poll**(2) and the **ioctl**(2) I_SETSIG command. These calls allow a user process to detect events that occur at the Stream head on one or more Streams, including receipt of a data or protocol message on the read queue and cessation of flow control.

Synchronous monitoring is provided by use of **poll** alone; in this case, the user process cannot continue processing until after the system call completes. When the calls are used together, they allow asynchronous, or concurrent, operation of the process and STREAMS input/output. This allows the user process to monitor the Stream while carrying on other activities.

To monitor Streams with **poll**, a user process issues that system call and specifies the Streams to be monitored, the events to look for, and the amount of time to wait for an event. **poll** will block the process until the time expires or until an event occurs. If an event occurs, **poll** will return the type of event and the Stream on which the event occurred.

Instead of waiting for an event to occur, a user process may want to monitor one or more Streams while processing other data. It can do so by issuing the **ioctl** I_SETSIG command, specifying one or more Streams and events (as with **poll**). Unlike a **poll**, this **ioctl** does not force the user process to wait for the event but returns immediately and will issue a signal when an event occurs. The process must also request **signal**(2) or **sigset**(2) to catch the resultant SIGPOLL signal.

If any selected event occurs on any of the selected Streams, STREAMS will cause the SIGPOLL catching function to be executed in all associated requesting processes. However, the process(es) will not know which event occurred, nor on what Stream the event occurred. A process that issues the I_SETSIG can get more detailed information by issuing a **poll** after it detects the event.

Error and Trace Logging

STREAMS includes error and trace loggers useful for debugging and administering modules and drivers.

Any module or driver in any Stream can call the STREAMS logging function **strlog**, described in **log**(7). When called, **strlog** will send formatted text to the error logger **strerr**(1M), the trace logger **strace**(1M), or both. The call parameters for **strlog** include the module/driver identification, a severity level, and the formatted text describing the condition causing the call. The call also identifies the process (**strerr** and/or **strace**) to receive the resultant output message.

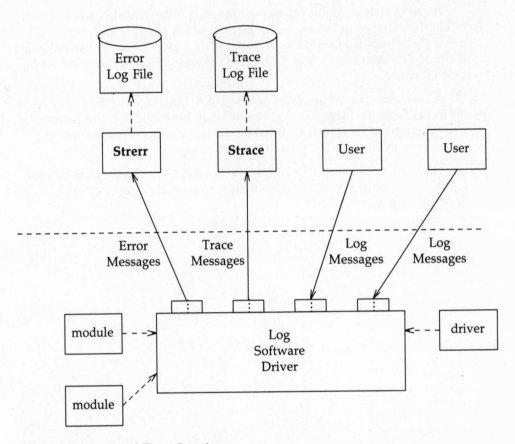

Figure 6-5: Error and Trace Logging

strerr is intended to operate as a daemon process initiated at system startup. A call to **strlog** requesting an error to be logged causes an M_PROTO message to be sent to **strerr**, which formats the contents and places them in a daily file. The utility **strclean**(1M) is provided to periodically purge aged, unreferenced daily log files.

A call to **strlog** requesting trace information to be logged causes a similar M_PROTO message to be sent to **strace**(1M), which places it in a user designated file. **strace** is intended to be initiated by a user. The user can designate the modules/drivers and severity level of the messages to be accepted for logging by **strace**.

A user process can submit its own M_PROTO messages to the log driver for inclusion in the logger of its choice through **putmsg**(2). The messages must be in the same format required by the logging processes and will be switched to the logger(s) requested in the message.

The output to the log files is formatted, ASCII text. The files can be processed by standard system commands such as **grep**(1) or **ed**(1), or by developer-provided routines.

7 DRIVER DESIGN COMPARISONS

Introduction

This chapter compares operational features of character I/O device drivers with STREAMS drivers and modules. It is intended for experienced developers of UNIX system character device drivers. Details are provided in the *STREAMS Programmer's Guide*.

Environment

No user environment is generally available to STREAMS module procedures and drivers. The exception is the module and driver open and close routines, both of which have access to the u_area of the calling process and can sleep. Otherwise, a STREAMS driver, module put procedure, and module service procedure has no user context and can neither sleep nor access any u_area.

Multiple Streams can use a copy of the same module (that is, the same **fmodsw**), each containing the same processing procedures. This means that module code is reentrant, so care must be exercised when using global data in a module. Put and service procedures are always passed the address of the QUEUE (for example, in Figure 2-5 Au calls Bu's put procedure with Bu as a parameter). The processing procedure establishes its environment solely from the QUEUE contents, typically the private data (for example, state information).

Drivers

At the interface to hardware devices, character I/O drivers have interrupt entry points; at the system interface, those same drivers generally have direct entry points (routines) to process **open**, **close**, **read**, **write** and **ioctl** system calls.

STREAMS device drivers have similar interrupt entry points at the hardware device interface and have direct entry points only for **open** and **close** system calls. These entry points are accessed via STREAMS, and the call formats differ from character device drivers. The put procedure is a driver's third entry point, but it is a message (not system) interface. The Stream head translates **write** and **ioctl** calls into messages and sends them downstream to

be processed by the driver's write QUEUE put procedure. **read** is seen directly only by the Stream head, which contains the functions required to process system calls. A driver does not know about system interfaces other than **open** and **close**, but it can detect absence of a **read** indirectly if flow control propagates from the Stream head to the driver and affects the driver's ability to send messages upstream.

For input processing, when the driver is ready to send data or other information to a user process, it does not wake up the process. It prepares a message and sends it to the read QUEUE of the appropriate (minor device) Stream. The driver's open routine generally stores the QUEUE address corresponding to this Stream.

For output processing, the driver receives messages in place of a **write** call. If the message can not be sent immediately to the hardware, it may be stored on the driver's write message queue. Subsequent output interrupts can remove messages from this queue.

Drivers and modules can pass signals, error codes, and return values to processes via message types provided for that purpose.

Modules

As described above, modules have user context available only during the execution of their open and close routines. Otherwise, the QUEUEs forming the module are not associated with the user process at the end of the Stream, nor with any other process. Because of this, QUEUE procedures must not sleep when they cannot proceed; instead, they must explicitly return control to the system. The system saves no state information for the QUEUE. The QUEUE must store this information internally if it is to proceed from the same point on a later entry.

When a module or driver that requires private working storage (for example, for state information) is pushed, the open routine must obtain the storage from external sources. STREAMS copies the module template from **fmodsw** for the I_PUSH, so only fixed data can be contained in the module template. STREAMS has no automatic mechanism to allocate working storage to a module when it is opened. The sources for the storage typically include a module-specific kernel array, installed when the system is configured, or the STREAMS buffer pool. When using an array as a module storage pool, the maximum number of copies of the module that can exist at any one time must be determined. For drivers, this is typically determined from the physical

devices connected, such as the number of ports on a multiplexor. However, certain types of modules may not be associated with a particular external physical limit. For example, the CANONICAL module shown in Figure 2-4 could be used on different types of Streams.

Introduction ───

Glossary

downstream   The direction from Stream head to driver.

driver   The end of the Stream closest to an external interface. The principal functions of the driver are handling any associated device, and transforming data and information between the external interface and Stream. It can also be a pseudo-driver, not directly associated with a device, which performs functions internal to a Stream, such as a multiplexor or log driver.

message   One or more linked blocks of data or information, with associated STREAMS control structures containing a message type. Messages are the only means of transferring data and communicating within a Stream.

message queue   A linked list of messages connected to a QUEUE.

message type   A defined set of values identifying the contents of a message.

module   Software that performs functions on messages as they flow between Stream head and driver. A module is the STREAMS counterpart to the commands in a Shell pipeline except that a module contains a pair of functions which allow independent bidirectional (downstream and upstream) data flow and processing.

multiplexor   A mechanism for connecting multiple Streams to a multiplexing driver. The mechanism supports the processing of interleaved data Streams and the processing of internetworking protocols. The multiplexing driver routes messages among the connected Streams. The other end of a Stream connected to a multiplexing driver is typically connected to a device driver.

pushable module   A module between the Stream head and driver. A driver is a non-pushable module and a Stream head includes a non-pushable module.

QUEUE

The set of structures that forms a module. A module is composed of two QUEUEs, a read (upstream) QUEUE and a write (downstream) QUEUE.

read queue

The message queue in a module or driver containing messages moving upstream. Associated with input from a driver.

Stream

The kernel aggregate created by connecting STREAMS components, resulting from an application of the STREAMS mechanism. The primary components are a Stream head, a driver and zero or more pushable modules between the Stream head and driver. A Stream forms a full duplex processing and data transfer path in the kernel, between a user process and a driver. A Stream is analogous to a Shell pipe-line except that data flow and processing are bidirectional.

Stream head

The end of the Stream closest to the user process. The Stream head provides the interface between the Stream and the user process. The principal functions of the Stream head are processing STREAMS-related system calls, and bidirectional transfer of data and information between a user process and messages in STREAMS' kernel space.

STREAMS

A kernel mechanism that supports development of network services and data communication drivers. It defines interface standards for character input/output within the kernel, and between the kernel and user level. The STREAMS mechanism comprises integral functions, utility routines, kernel facilities and a set of structures.

upstream

The direction from driver to Stream head.

write queue

The message queue in a module or driver containing messages moving downstream. Associated with output from a user process.